W9-AMU-877

pocket
supersex

pocket supersex

tracey cox

DK Publishing Inc.

LONDON, NEW YORK, MUNICH, MELBOURNE, AND DELHI

Design
XAB Design
Senior Editor
Peter Jones
Senior Art Editor
Hannah Moore
Category Publisher
Corinne Roberts
Art Director
Carole Ash
DTP Designer
Karen Constanti
Production Controller
Sarah Sherlock
Production Manager
Lauren Britton
Jacket Editor
Carrie Love
Jacket Designer
Nicola Powling

First American Edition, 2004

Published in the United States by
DK Publishing, Inc. 375 Hudson Street
New York, New York 10014

07 08 10 9 8 7 6 5 4 3 2

Copyright © 2004 Dorling Kindersley Limited
Text copyright © 2004 Tracey Cox

A Cataloging-in-Publication record for this
book is available from the Library of
Congress.

ISBN 978-0-7566-0516-2

Reproduced by GRB, Italy
Printed and bound by Star Standard,
Singapore

Discover more at
www.dk.com

contents

There's sex. There's good sex. **And there's supersex.** I'm talking the **toe-curling**, spine-tingling, **sell-the-kids-for-more variety.**

Introduction

I've always said big isn't necessarily best—and that's why the original *supersex* now comes packaged in a handy little pocket size. Small enough to slip into a suitcase for that naughty weekend away, it's nevertheless packed with ideas and saucy suggestions, so you can have supersex wherever you are!

> If you look after **your sex life**, **the love part** will look after itself.

Like the full-size version, *pocket supersex* aims both to inspire and troubleshoot—because, let's be honest here, most long-term relationships need a bit of both. No one (least of all me!) said it's easy having great sex with the same person for the rest of your life. But it can be done, and this book's going to help you do it.

Hopefully, you'll find it a fascinating flick-through for all kinds of reasons. It's got lots of quotes, raunchy parts, and trivia that you can drag out at dinner parties when you feel like being a show-off. It's a little naughty in parts, downright dirty in others, and unashamedly slanted toward encouraging everyone to adopt a healthy, if-it-feels-good-do-it attitude to sex.

Whether you're heterosexual, metrosexual, bisexual, single, married, with kids or without, this book will help to enhance your sex life and relationship in general. (If you look after your sex life, the love part will look after itself.) It gave me great pleasure to write *pocket supersex*. I hope it will bring you great pleasure as well. In all senses of the word, enjoy!

Tracey X

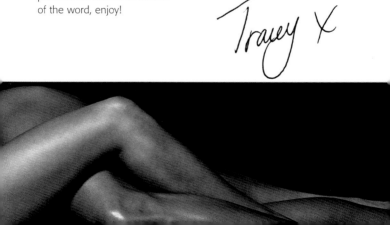

1 Hands on!

We tend to think oral sex and intercourse are superior, but the humble hand-job has several advantages over the competition.

Feeling fat and unattractive? You don't need to remove your clothes and get naked to give him what he's asking for. Got your period? If you're squeamish but horny, leave the tampon in and let him give you an orgasm using his fingers on your clitoris. Engrossed in a naughty movie and want to do it and her simultaneously? Keep those eyes glued to the screen and let your fingers do the walking. You don't need condoms because it's almost totally safe sex (unless you've got cuts on your hands/penis/vagina, the risk of passing on infection is extremely low). It's a great way of dabbling sexually with a new partner until you're ready for the intimacy of oral sex or penetration.

And you're much more likely to get away with doing it in public: he's driving and stuck in traffic/you're on a plane with her, a blanket over both your laps. Hands-on sex also paves the way for other diversionary delights. If his penis is starting to feel left out, invite him in to play. The head is wonderfully soft and ideal for stimulating the ultra-sensitive clitoris. (It's softer than a baby's bottom—I swear it!) Use your hands to guide it up and down, stroking over the entire clitoral area for a high-voltage, velvety vibe! A hand down our pants evokes innocent but sexy memories of Sam or Cindy behind the bleachers at school and, last but not least, a hand-job feels heavenly. With one hand on your genitals, another caressing elsewhere, a tongue in your mouth, and lips pressed against yours, you're drowning in a sea of sensations because you're getting it from all sides, all at once. Ready to revamp an old classic into your New Favorite Thing? Try this…

> ## This won't just **take him to heaven**; he'll be driven there by a **big-busted blonde** in a **Ferrari**.

HIS TURN

Alex Comfort (a.k.a. Mr. *Joy of Sex*) says a woman who knows how to masturbate a man "subtly, unhurriedly, and mercilessly" will almost always make a superlative partner. I thoroughly agree—and suspect Mr. Comfort would approve of this step-by-step guide.

- **Uh, how do I do this again?** Don't be embarrassed to admit that you don't have a clue about what you're doing—he'll be more than happy to demonstrate. Unlike some holier-than-thou women who claim they can't show their boyfriends how they like to be touched because they've never masturbated (wide eyes, batting lashes—oh puhleeze!), you'd be hard-pressed to find a man who won't admit he's been doing it since age seven. Get him to show you what rhythm, speed, and pressure he likes by putting your hand over his as he masturbates himself. When you think you've got it right, swap hands so your hand's now underneath and his is on top. Ask for feedback. If he's too shy, spoon-feed him by asking: "harder?/ faster?/slower?" and look for a nod or shake of the head.

- **Use lubricant** Sometimes a combination of saliva and pre-ejaculatory fluid (the stuff that comes out before orgasm when he's excited) is enough to keep things nice and slippery. It's always a good idea though to keep a tube of personal lubricant near the bed. A dry hand-job is OK. A wet one won't just take him to heaven; he'll be driven there by a big-busted blonde in a Ferrari.

- **Get comfy** Forget lying beside him on the bed. Instead, straddle his chest and face toward his penis, or get him to kneel on the bed in front of you, or stand in front of the bed while you sit on it. All three positions mean you can use both hands without losing balance and touch other areas. Plus you'll be more inclined to take time and really spoil him if you're in a comfortable position.

- **The basic stroke** Use one hand to hold the penis steady, the other to slide up and down the shaft in a whole-hand, loose-fist movement, closing your fist gently but firmly as it slides up and over the head. The technique is roughly the same whether he's circumcised or not, but you've got more to work with if it's intact. Never, EVER, yank the foreskin back until he's properly lubricated (unless you *want* to cause him pain!). Use saliva or lubricant to make it nice and slippery, then gently ease the foreskin back and over the head of the penis. You can then work with the foreskin, sliding it up and over the head during the basic stroke.

- **Get the pressure right** Too gentle can feel like "nothing," but too firm HURTS!!!! If in doubt, start off being gentle and ask him if it's hard enough. It's easy to get a little carried away once you get into the swing of it. If you're starting to think of his penis as a big bendy plaything and at the point where you're wondering if you could twist it to make an animal, like they do with balloons, better stop right there! Penises are human flesh and—even more surprising— attached to an owner! (Yes, he is still there!)

● **Feel the rhythm** Start off s-l-o-w and t-e-a-s-i-n-g-l-y tortuous, then speed up as he moves toward orgasm. Going too fast too soon usually does one of two things (neither is fab): 1. He becomes insensitive to your touch; 2. He gets sore and oversensitive. A good hand-job is like a good movie. It starts off slow and interesting, then builds steadily to a glorious climax—with interesting twists and turns along the way.

● **My hand's about to fall off!** Removing both hands and massaging them while saying

"Owww!" and rocking back and forth isn't the sexiest sight in the world. Besides, you can't just leave him, well, hanging. Instead, give your fingers a rest by simply wrapping them around his penis, holding firm and holding still. Give each hand a rest in this way. Even if you're not feeling numb or tired, stopping for a minute or so can up the tension nicely, so don't feel guilty!

> **A good hand-job is like a good movie.** It starts off slow and interesting then builds steadily to a **glorious climax**—with **interesting twists** and turns along the way.

- **What now? Looks like he's about to…!** It's all individual, but most men prefer you to increase pressure and rhythm significantly the few seconds before orgasm and ejaculation, then slow it right down and go gentler during it. Just don't stop completely! After orgasm, a lot of men are ultrasensitive: that loving squeeze could have him shooting through the roof rather than leaning over for a smooch. Most importantly though…don't fuss over the cleanup. If I EVER catch ANY of you doing that girly, eeww-how-messy-is-this thing, your supersexpert status will be withdrawn immediately!

A TWIST ON THE USUAL

- **Be a pastry chef** Place his penis in between your two flat palms, fingers extended so that your hands are straight. Now roll them as if his penis were pastry. Great if he's having erection problems, yummy even if he's not.
- **Run rings around him** Make sure he's well-lubricated then make two rings around his penis with the thumb and index finger of each hand. Place them next to each other in the middle of the shaft, then continually slide in opposite directions simultaneously.
- **Play Twister** Triple the sensation of the basic stroke by twisting your hand as you reach the part where the head meets the shaft. This applies extra stimulation to the frenulum (the area of puckered skin on the underside of the penis), which is packed with nerve endings and is supersensitive.
- **The mini-massage** Here, you're using the same technique you would to massage his back but on a much smaller area. Start with both thumbs placed in the middle of the base of his penis on the underside (the side closest to his testicles). Now gently push your thumbs, massaging upward and outward, always returning to the center and working up the shaft as you go.
- **Tease please** Build up to a constant rhythm, then every few minutes slow it right down and ease the pressure to frustratingly light for the count of 10. Repeat the whole thing at least four times.
- **Pull his hair** Tug gently but rhythmically on his pubic hair, starting by gently pulling a few strands between your thumb and forefinger, then pulling larger amounts. Because his penis extends inside, as well as out, this massages the internal part.

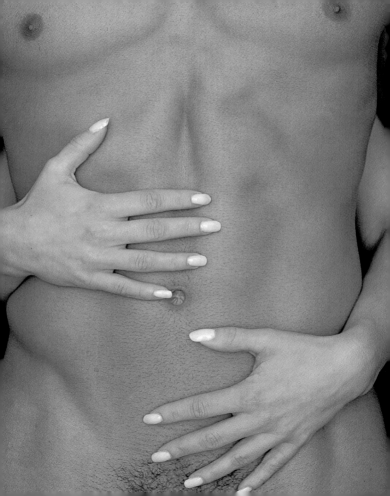

HER TURN

Men are usually better at giving hand-jobs to women because they've had more practice: all that time at "second base," trying desperately to turn their girlfriend on so she'll finally give in and go "all the way" has paid off. If you're still a little uncertain, take a tip from Britain's bad boy, *FHM* magazine's sexpert Grub Smith. He instructs his male readers to "do everything half as fast and twice as softly as you think you should." Keep this as your hands-on mantra, combine it with the following tips, and you won't go wrong.

- **Leave her hat on** Double the delight by leaving her clothes on for as long as possible. Fondle and stroke her breasts through a sheer slippery bra before moving on to stroke her clitoris through sexy panties. Not only does it give her even more incentive to invest in grrrreat lingerie (seems worth it if it's not ripped off immediately), but it's also a huge turn-on when you finally do push aside the material to touch naked flesh.
- **The warm up** Before you even think about paddling toward the little man in the boat (the clitoris, in case you're wondering), try cupping the whole vulva (genital area) through her clothes and gently applying even, circular pressure. Keep the fabric of her panties between you, then try placing your first and middle fingers in between her labia lips lengthwise and vibrating them in a gentle scissor motion.
- **Get into position** The usual technique involves reaching one hand down while kissing or lying beside her. A far more practical—albeit not as romantic—position is to sit facing her between her open legs, while she's either sitting or lying back with her knees up. Try her positioned on a chair/the side of the bed/kitchen counter, with you kneeling or sitting in front.

- **Stroke her thighs** One at a time—fingers splayed and trailing up her inner thighs then over her vagina but not lingering—then use both hands to stroke up both thighs simultaneously. Keep going until her legs open wider and wider and it's obvious she wants you to center on her genital region.
- **Let her do the work** Start by holding your fingers against her closed labia and pay attention to how she positions herself and grinds against you. This is your clue to where she wants you to concentrate and how much pressure she requires. At all times her

> Do everything
> **half as fast** and **twice as softly**
> as you think you should.

hip movements—how fast and how furiously she grinds them against your hand—are your guide to the pressure and speed she's craving. If she's not grinding against your hand at all, you're either doing it perfectly (gold star!) or she's unsure of how you'll react if she gives you feedback. All the more reason to…

- **Ask for help** While reading her hip movements helps, if you think she's up for it, it's even better to ask her to show you how she masturbates herself. The usual lesson you'll learn from this if she obliges: it's better to run your finger around the clitoris than stimulate it directly. While we're on the topic, just as you hate her grabbing straight for the crown jewels, it's also a really, really bad idea to ignore the labia lips and rush straight for the main attraction: the clitoris. If the clitoris is stimulated too early, too hard, or too soon, the reaction you'll get is more likely to be pain than pleasure.

- **Getting technical** OK, now we're ready to (ahem) dive straight in. But first, test how lubricated she is by gently running one finger along the crease of the labia lips. Don't be put off if she's not sliding off the bed already. It could mean you're not turning her on or that you need to prolong foreplay, although everything from taking the Pill to having a yeast infection can affect how wet she is. Quite often, the lubrication is there, it's just trapped inside. If you gently insert a fingertip inside the vagina, you can spread the lubrication around (but not directly on) the clitoris.

- **Go for it** This is a variation on the "cupping" we did earlier. Place your palm over her pubic hair and bend your middle finger so it's angled to touch her clitoris. Cup her pubic area and use your finger to rub her clitoris up and down or in circles. Slide the two fingers next to it alongside so they stimulate the edges of the labia. Next, use your middle finger to make circles or figure eights around the clitoris. Your main stroke now involves touching and rubbing the shaft of the clitoris—the bit behind the clitoral hood (the skin which protects and covers the clitoris). Although most action does center around the clitoris, it's a rare woman who can cope with direct and prolonged stimulation on it.

- **The two golden rules** Rule No 1: DON'T change technique, especially when she's heading straight for the "Oooooowwwwweeeeeeee" stage. You think showing off an infinite variety of hand twirls will result in her saying, "Wow! You know so many ways to use your fingers! What a star!" It won't. She'll fix you with a look of rage and/or frustration (probably both) and say

"What were you trying to prove? If you'd just kept on doing it the one way, it would have worked. Why did you have to be such a show-off?" Well, even if she smiles sweetly and pretends to be happy, believe me—that's what she wanted to say. So think one method, one speed. The only thing that should interrupt the flow is if she's not flowing: the one thing she won't mind you stopping for is to lubricate the area. In case you hadn't guessed, that's Rule No 2: Keep things wet. It's impossible for her to be too wet, but oh-so-easy to be too dry. The minute you feel lubrication starting to dry up, add more. Another dollop of lubricant or loads of saliva.

● **But what happened to bringing her to orgasm simply by thrusting inside with my fingers?** Indeed! Women don't usually masturbate by thrusting a finger in and out of their vaginas, so not much point in you trying to make them orgasm by using just the same technique, is there boys? Combine it with clitoral stimulation if you really want to tip her over the edge.

2 Oh. My. God.

Find the person whose mouth makes the right moves and join the line of those eager to lap up the attention. The opposite also applies: refuse to get up close and personal and don't be surprised if your dance card stays empty.

Why? Oral sex is not just one of life's great pleasures—our attitude to it also speaks volumes about our attitude to sex in general. Open, uninhibited, sensuous lovers adore both giving and receiving oral sex. Prissy, uptight, and why-would-you-possibly-want-to-go-there are adjectives that apply to the rest. Eager to learn a few more tricks to add to your repertoire? You'll find a couple here. Your grandmother probably told you the way to a lover's heart was through his stomach. Well, try heading south a bit. There are guides for both of you, but ladies first…

THE LICK OF LOVE: MAGICAL MOUTH TECHNIQUES FOR HER

Trim and terrific Encourage her to trim any excess pubic hair or have it waxed. The less hair around the clitoris, the greater the pleasure for the both of you (coughing up an errant hair like a cat with a fur ball isn't sexy). While she's doing her part, do yours by shaving just before you nuzzle around down there. Stubble leaves a rash and it hurts.

Don't take a nosedive Ripping back the covers and diving straight for it isn't a turn-on. Anticipation is everything. Work your way down her body—kissing, nibbling, licking nipples, tummy, thighs—and make her wait. Her hips should be straining upward in a (vain) attempt to hurry things up before you take it any further. Like, you're oh-so-close it's ridiculous. And while we're on the subject of being up-close and personal, a healthy vagina shouldn't smell unpleasant. If hers does, she may have an infection or need to make some dietary adjustments. Which is why a garlic-laden dinner à deux in that romantic French restaurant isn't such a great idea if you want to do more than just hold hands afterward. Yup, it doesn't just show up on her breath.

> According to **some sexperts**, **one side of the clitoris** is often more pleasure-prone than the other.

Get a head start Let her demonstrate which tongue technique she'd like you to use by getting her to lick your palm the way she'd like you to lick her. She'll probably use the whole flat of her tongue rather than a tensed tip, and wiggle and swish in a slow, lazy, large movement.

Power positions
- **Her on top:** instead of her lying back and you lying between her legs, you lie back on the bed and get her to climb on top of you, facing the headboard. She puts her hands against the wall behind the bed to steady herself, then lowers onto your mouth and tongue. This gives her complete control over the pressure: she can

lift away from your mouth if it's too rough, move closer if she wants it harder. Your neck's not cramped and it keeps your tongue from getting tired. (A comfort tip for other positions: if she's on her side you can rest your head on her thigh.)

● **Through the roof:** she lies back on the bed, you kneel between her legs, then you lift them up so they're resting on your shoulders. You're in a kneeling position, she's lifted in the air, her shoulders still on the bed. She uses her hands to support herself, plus you're supporting her by holding her legs. This feels fantastic and she gets the added turn-on of seeing exactly what's going on.

Keep it covered Get her to leave her panties on and start by licking through the fabric. (Yes, it helps if she's wearing satin or silk, rather than the graying, thick cotton numbers.) Instead of removing them completely to finish the job, pull them to one side. This will transport her straight back to her first oral experiences (when she was young, trying hard to be good—and failing spectacularly).

Making mouth music Separate the vaginal lips with your fingers, find her clitoris (a tiny marble, at the top end—the end near her tummy—covered with a hood of skin), and make gentle, slow, upward strokes around the clitoris, not on it. Remember the movement she showed you on your palm? Use the flat of your tongue, not the tip. Keep your tongue relaxed; it'll feel better for her, and you won't get so tired. Make slow circles around the circumference and combine this with an up-and-down, lapping motion. Let as much of your tongue make contact so you cover the largest area possible. Practice on your own palm and see which movements feel most efficient. If you see her clitoris shrinking or retracting back under the hood of skin, you're being too rough.

Direct directions When you're in position, it's difficult to interpret anything but moaning and the most simple sentences. After all, her legs are covering your ears and emerging to ask "What did you say?" isn't ideal when it was "For God's sake, don't stop because I'm just about to…." Ask her to use single-word instructions like "lighter," "harder," "perfect." She may also use body language to show you what she wants. If she pulls your head closer or rises up to meet you, she wants you to go harder. If she's wriggling away, you're being too rough or too fast.

V marks the spot If you're having trouble hitting the hot spot, ask her to guide you to the right place by forming a "V" with her fingers, positioning them where she wants you to focus and then lick between them.

Take sides According to some sexperts, one side of the clitoris is often more pleasure-prone than the other. See if this holds true for her: make her clitoris more accessible by getting her to keep her left leg bent at the knee and angled outward while straightening the right one so it's in line with her body.
Then switch legs.

Write a love letter Use your tongue like a pen and "write" on her clitoris, spelling out each letter of whatever sentences you've made up in your head. This ensures you're varying your movements and means you won't overstimulate one particular area.

Bring up the rear Spread your hands wide and take a firm grip of her bottom. Squeeze and start rotating in big, wide circles. This feels good because it indirectly stimulates the anal area—a highly sensitive

Lots of women stay dead-still during orgasm. **Others gyrate** like they're **lap-dancing for Latvia.** Keep going regardless. Many men stop licking at **the crucial moment** thinking it's all over.

area for women as well as men, but one which some are a little shy about admitting to. This does the job, without her feeling uncomfortable. (Plenty of women aren't shy and like a finger inserted into their anus as well as vagina on orgasm, but ask first and use lots of lubricant.)

Don't be a show-off Switching techniques might score you points in the early stages, but stick to one technique as she approaches orgasm.

Lift off Increase the speed and pressure but keep on doing whatever it is you're doing and keep the rhythm regular. Lots of

I HATE GIVING ORAL SEX! DO I REALLY HAVE TO DO IT?

The short answer is yes. Refuse to give a guy oral sex and he has every right to get it elsewhere (and the same applies to you). It's one of the most pleasurable aspects of sex and to deny him it and expect him to remain faithful is unthinkable. Besides, there are three main reasons why women don't like giving men oral sex. Happily, each has a very simple solution...

- **It smells** Have a shower together beforehand or ask him to. Make sure he pulls back the foreskin and washes underneath.

- **I gag** Change your position and technique for maximum control. Get him to stand in front of you while you sit on the bed facing him. Use one hand to control his penis, placing it at the bottom of the shaft, and you're now in the ultimate position to control how deeply you take him into your mouth. Most feeling is in the head of the penis, not the shaft, so you don't need to go too deep. If he does that charming hands-behind-your-head-to-shove-you-down-farther thing, tell him if he does it again, you won't just stop immediately but permanently. That's fixed that problem then.

- **Swallowing makes me want to throw up** If you don't want to swallow, don't! Instead, continue stimulating him with your hand and let him ejaculate elsewhere on your body. Contrary to popular belief, semen is not sulfuric acid, although you'd think it was, considering the way some women go on about it! It tastes a little like alfalfa sprouts that still have some dirt clinging to them—not exactly chocolate, but hardly disgusting. (And if his is, he needs to look at his diet and cut out the beer, fries, spicy food, and garlic.) Another trick if you don't like the taste: swallow it quickly and in one shot, the way you do medicine.

women stay dead-still during orgasm. Others gyrate like they're lap-dancing for Latvia. Keep going regardless. Our orgasms last a long time and many men stop licking at the crucial moment, thinking it's all over. Well, it may be for you if you get it wrong! Keep on with slow, gentle strokes until she pushes you away. (Which she may do because the clitoris gets extremely sensitive after orgasm, so don't be offended!)

> **Ripping back the covers** and diving straight for it isn't a turn-on. **Anticipation is everything.** Work your way down her body—kissing, nibbling, licking nipples, tummy, thighs—**and make her wait.**

BLOW HIS...MIND: TIPS AND TRICKS TO TAKE HIM TO HEAVEN

The visual feast Leave the lights on so he can see what you're doing. Give him real front-seat action by tying your hair back as well. If you're brave, hold eye contact while you're fellating him; if you're too embarrassed, look at his penis instead.

Position-plus

● He stands, you sit facing him on the side of the bed (or any piece of furniture of appropriate height). It's more comfortable for both of you and it leaves your hands free to stimulate his penis, nipples, testicles, perineum, etc. without getting hand cramps. It also gives you control over how deeply he thrusts into your mouth. Some men say their legs go all weak after orgasm but most can survive if they collapse on the bed immediately afterward!

● He stands, you kneel in front of him. It's more comfortable than lying down beside him, though the chief appeal is being in the classic "submissive" pose. (If being on your knees reeks so much of subservience that your feminist friends would never forgive you, ditch the friends, not the position!)

Use your tongue like a pen and **"write" on her clitoris**, spelling out whatever sentences you've made up.

But not yet… Lick your way downward until his penis is straining for attention, then bypass it completely by licking down the outside of his thighs until you reach the inside of his knee, then move back up his inner thigh until you get to his testicles. Stop right there and drive him nuts, using large tongue movements to swirl around each testicle.

Add hands Get the hand motion under control before you add your mouth. Don't tug or yank at the foreskin; manipulate it so it slides up and over the head and, again, remember to keep things nice and slippery. Use your hands, not your mouth, to control his penis and always use two hands. One holds the penis so it doesn't move all over the place, the other touches him elsewhere. It also takes the pressure off—literally—if you alternate between two kinds of stimulation simultaneously.

Liquid licks Before you head downward, let lots of saliva pool in your mouth (sorry, far too much information I know, but I did promise to tell you everything!). It really can't be too wet for him inside there, so keep some water close by if your mouth gets dry. The more lubricated he is, the more pleasurable it will feel.

Oral action Lower for a lollipop lick—one fabulously long lick

Contrary to popular belief, **semen is not sulfuric acid**, although you'd think it was the way some women go on about it! It **tastes** a little **like alfafa sprouts**—not quite chocolate, but hardly disgusting.

from the base of his penis right to the top—then make an "O," and in one movement, slide your mouth over his erection, taking him as far in as is comfortable. Move from there into the bread-and-butter stroke: with one hand, grip the bottom of the shaft while you slide your mouth up and down. The basic hand movement stays the same: slide your hand up and down, closing it when you reach the head, opening it slightly as you slide down the length. Establish a regular fellatio rhythm, then move into the twist-and-swirl. Make a twisting motion with one hand as you're sliding up and down and swirl your tongue around the rim of the head, paying particular attention to the frenulum (the bit of skin on the underside of his penis).

Access all areas Keep stimulating other areas while you're fellating him. Try firmly stroking (or massaging in mini-circles) the perineum (the area between his anus and testicles). Tickle and stroke the area below his belly button and the base of his penis just as he's about to orgasm.

On the home run As with women, it's important that you maintain a steady rhythm to build excitement. As he approaches orgasm, however, step up the speed and pressure.

The fellatio finale If you don't want to finish him off in your

When you're in position, it's difficult to interpret **anything but moaning** and the most simple sentences. After all, her **legs are covering** your ears and emerging to ask "What did you say?" isn't ideal.

mouth, switch to intercourse just before the crucial moment. The next best thing to you swallowing: using your hands to masturbate him and letting him orgasm over your breasts.

My pleasure Now all that's left to do is…lie back and wait for the congratulations. They should follow immediately after he's finished moaning "Oh. My. God." about 25 times.

3 Penis genius

All the most interesting stuff that even he doesn't know about his most precious part.

Want to see some naked breasts? You'll find exactly what you're looking for in virtually any tabloid, most magazines, and lots of films. Wanna see a naked penis? Sorry, you'll have to hide out in a public bathroom for that one. While garden variety, celebrity, and even royal breasts are everywhere, not even Joe-ordinary penises are caught swaying in the breeze. In most countries and in most conservative mediums, it's illegal to show an erect penis, unless it's attached to a Burmese bumble-bee on the National Geographic channel. Which is a shame really, since a truly erect, so-hard-it's-going-to-burst, veins-throbbing, blood-pumping penis is a rather glorious and gladiatorial sight!

You can show a flaccid penis if there's a good—i.e. educational—reason for it. But even men tend to agree that nonerect penises look faintly ridiculous and sort of pointless just dangling there, not really doing anything (like God had a little modeling clay left over and decided to played a joke after rolling it up into a sausage). Hardly surprising, then, that most men aren't jumping up and down saying "Pick me! Pick me!" for the chance to show theirs off in that state. One reason why females are rarely treated to a public sighting.

Men, on the other hand, get plenty of chances to compare their whatnots against everybody else's. Hence the paranoia. If female fears over genitalia aren't helped by the fact that we can't see our genitals properly without using a mirror, men's are probably due to being able to see theirs and other men's equipment in the urinals and communal shower far too frequently and making too many, often inaccurate, comparisons. (And here's three instantly gratifying

> Why does **one testicle hang lower** than the other? It stops them from **getting squashed** when he walks! None of us have symmetrical bodies and in **85 percent of males** it's the left testicle that's **lower and larger.**

reassurances for the truly unnerved before I go any further: 1. A cylindrical object always appears longer and bigger when viewed from the side than when seen from above; 2. Actors in porn films aren't the norm: they're specifically hired because of their abnormally large penis size; 3. The entrance to the vagina—the first third— is more sensitive than the last two-thirds. Further proof that length really doesn't matter. Feeling better already? Fab! Now, read on...)

Bernie Zilbergeld (acclaimed sex therapist and author of *The New Male Sexuality*) got it right when he said penis envy does exist...within the male population. While good old (sexist, paranoid,

FACT 1

MYTH: Having sex the night before affects his athletic performance.

REALITY: In a recent study, men who had sex the night before a strenuous workout suffered no serious decreases in strength, balance, reaction time, or cardiovascular power the next day. In fact, it might just improve his game because sex relieves prematch stress and tension.

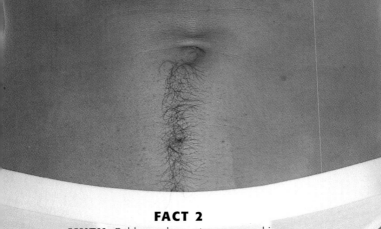

FACT 2

MYTH: Bald guys have stronger sex drives.
REALITY: Probably true. The myth says bald men
are more virile than men with hair because they
have more testosterone in their bodies (which
can cause hair loss). The testosterone/
hair-loss link is true and
testosterone is indeed the
chemical responsible
for his sexual
libido.

delusional) Sigmund Freud might have coined the term to explain why women envy men their dangly parts, but the fact is that most don't (except possibly when desperate to go pee outdoors).

Sadly, these days penis envy rings true for a different reason: namely, that most men seem to want to trade their penis for someone else's. One that is wider, harder, bigger, longer, and has more staying power than their own. Only one thing stops these men from ever realizing their dream of owning the longed-for highly prized Deluxe Model—

A **high testosterone level** can get you in trouble. Married men who test **above average are more likely to have affairs** and (no guesses why) are more likely to **end up divorced.**

and it's not penis transplant surgery. The Deluxe Model, blessed with all these qualities, only really exists in their imagination. No other part of the male body is more shrouded in myth and folklore than his most precious body part. So, in an attempt to sort the fact from the fiction, to reassure, and—OK, I admit it—simply to entertain, over these and the next few pages, you'll find a selection of stats and snippets, details and data to sort the fact from the fictitious. Not only will it turn both of you into instant penis geniuses (and make you a huge hit at dinner parties), it's also guaranteed to make his head swell. In all the right places.

STIFF COMPETITION

- Despite size differences when flaccid, most penises are around the same size when erect. (Some penises actually double in length.)
- Average erect size range: 5–6in (13–15cm). Flaccid size range: 2–4in (5–10cm).
- Smallest functional penis recorded on a man: ⅝in (1.8cm).
- Largest functional penis recorded on a man: 11in (28cm).
- Average gain in size after penile enlargement surgery: when flaccid, 3in (7.6cm); erect, 1in (2.5cm).

There's **more protein in an average ejaculation** than in a medium-sized pork chop. Choose to **swallow rather than spit** and you've provided your body with a large part of your **daily dose** of protein!

- Amount of blood in a flaccid penis: 3oz (9ml); amount in erect penis: 30oz (90ml).
- Just 3 percent of American men measure less than 4in (10cm) when erect; while 6 percent of American men measure just under 10in (25cm).
- Men with large testicles are more likely to cheat on their partners and to have 30 percent more sex than men with smaller testicles. (Levels of testosterone are higher in men with larger testicles.)

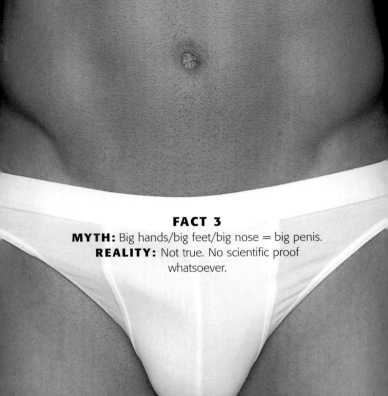

FACT 3
MYTH: Big hands/big feet/big nose = big penis.
REALITY: Not true. No scientific proof
whatsoever.

FACT 4

MYTH: Black guys are bigger.

REALITY: Yup. And their penises are thicker, too.
The Journal of Research in Personality studied
Asian, Caucasian, and black men and came
up with the following results: Asian men
are smallest, averaging 4–5½in
(10–14cm); Caucasians are
next, at 6in (15cm);
then black men,
at 6¼–8in
(16–20cm).

GOING UP?

- The average time a man can keep an erection: 40 minutes. The younger the man, the longer he can keep it up.
- Average speed of ejaculation: 28 mph (45 kph).
- Percentage of men who say they climax too early: 30.
- Average number of erections per day for a man: seven. Average number of erections that occur while he's asleep: five.
- The penis has a safety valve to ensure that a man can't ejaculate and urinate at the same time.
- Only one-third of impotency cases are due to physical problems, and 90 percent are treatable.

Men's fears are caused by seeing other **men's equipment in the urinals** and communal shower and making too many **inaccurate comparisons.**

TRIVIAL PURSUITS

- According to researchers at Taiwan University, waiting too long to urinate can reduce blood flow to your heart by about 25 percent.
- Two in every thousand men are capable of giving themselves fellatio.
- The tissue that surrounds the penis is more durable than the tissue that surrounds the brain.
- The distance sperm travel to fertilize an egg: 3–4in (7.5–10cm). The human equivalent: 26 miles (42km).

BALL GAMES

- Testicles disappear when a man gets cold or as he approaches orgasm. It's a reflex action. They retract into his body during intercourse as a protective instinct, so they don't get knocked around. Testes also produce and care for semen, which must be kept at a constant temperature (lower than the rest of the body but not freezing), so testicles rise and fall against the body depending on how much heat they need. Hence all the hype about tight jeans or tight underwear, which hold the testes too close to the body, making men infertile. This is why the testes are stored away from the body in their own little custom-made carrier, the scrotum.

- Does the size of the testicles indicate fertility? Larger testicles produce more sperm but size doesn't affect quality. To produce vigorous sperm quit smoking, cut back on the booze, exercise lots, and eat well. That's right: the more boring (a.k.a. healthy) you are, the more likely you are to become a dad. (Consider it future training for all those nights at home once the little treasure arrives.)

- The largest testicles in the world belong to...your boyfriend. Nope. Wrong answer. It's the Northern White Whale, which—with testicles that can weigh up to 2,200lbs (990 kg)—wins the prize.

- The testes also produce the male sex hormone, testosterone. Testosterone levels peak early morning, which is—gosh! what a surprise!—when most men want sex the most.

- Zinc supplements or normal exercise increase supplies of testosterone. Stress or exhausting exercise decrease it. When testosterone levels run low, men become more irritable, depressed, and sleepy.

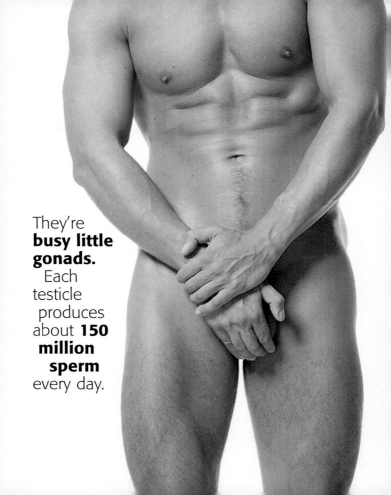

They're **busy little gonads.** Each testicle produces about **150 million sperm** every day.

4 Twelve sex tricks

Great sex takes time—but there are plenty of little tricks that'll get you there faster!

I asked 20 couples, all of whom described themselves as "above average" lovers, to test out the following techniques, which are designed to give an instant zing to your sex life. They rated them for enjoyment, and I took an average to give you a raunch rating. Of course, to be absolutely sure my math is correct, it's probably a very good idea for you to test each and every one of them yourselves…

1 STARTLE THE SENSES
For both of you They do it in movies (usually ones starring Sharon Stone), but few of us use ice cubes anywhere but in drinks. It's a shame really, because an ice-cold mouth pressed against hot genitals feels exquisite! Put a glass full of small ice cubes nearby when you're having sex and pop some in your mouth before you fellate him; insert one into her vagina before performing oral sex (not too big a cube though—you want to chill not numb). If ice cubes feel too startling, try chilled champagne, ice cream, or chilled, creamy yogurt instead. Next, raise the temperature all around by adding a hot drink and alternating the two sensations—a few minutes of stimulation by a cool mouth followed by a few minutes of stimulation by a hot mouth. Byrying

varying temperature and taste, you're activating two sets of nerve endings to serve up a sensory smorgasbord.

8/10 RAUNCHRATING RAUNCHRATING RAUNCHRATING RAUNCH

2 GIVE A HAND-JOB

For a different type of hand-job (but one that's equally as delicious) try the following:

For him Make him squirm in public by sucking his finger as though it's a small penis. Lean forward so no one else can see you (if you've got long hair, hide behind it), maintain eye contact, hold his finger in your mouth, and swirl and lick and suck until he can't take it any longer. Unless you're lavishly licking up and down his finger like it's a lollipop, it's relatively easy to get away with it without being arrested. In other words, keep most of the action happening inside your mouth (even if there is rather a lot happening in his jeans).

10/10 RAUNCHRATING RAUNCHRATING RAUNCHRATING RAUNCH

For her Return the public humiliation by lifting her hand to your mouth as though you're going to kiss the back of it, then turning it over and burying your tongue in her palm. As with the above, do like you'd do if you were giving her oral sex. Again, if you hold her hand at a right angle and keep most of the tongue action close, Aunt Betty could be watching and simply think you're being romantic. Well, she will until your girlfriend literally slides off her chair.

9/10 RAUNCHRATING RAUNCHRATING RAUNCHRATING RAUNCH

3 TELL A BEDTIME STORY

Forget Harry Potter, think Harry Does Sally.

For him Make up your own erotic tale or steal one of his girlie magazines and lift a story from the back. Lead him into the bedroom, tuck him into bed, sit by the bed on a chair, and open a book (any will do, since it's being used as a prop only). Then proceed to tell him the dirtiest, sexiest, most erotic fantasy scenario you can bear to say out loud. He's allowed to touch himself but not you. Let him masturbate himself to orgasm as you reach the climax of your tale.

For her Indulge a popular female fantasy: sex with a stranger. Blindfold her. Tie her hands behind her back. Lead her into a dark room and leave her standing alone for a few minutes. Then enter the room stealthily, come up behind her, and tell her you're the handsome stranger who's admired her from afar. She has a boyfriend but she's arranged to meet you, her unknown admirer, in a hotel room.

4 TURN OFF THE LIGHTS

For both of you After years of working up to having sex with all the lights on (yes, it takes most men that long to convince us they're not looking at the cellulite on our butts or the flab on our tummies), I'm now suggesting you not only turn the lights off but also make the room as close to total darkness as possible. Then blindfold each other. Why? By removing the sense of sight, you heighten all others—particularly touch and sensation. (It's the reason why lots of us close our eyes while kissing or during sex, so we can focus fully on the sensation.) Robbed of our eyesight, we're also more aware of each other's breathing and moaning and all the other sounds of sex, which tend to get lost when we can see. Yet another bonus: there's an element of surprise. Once your lover breaks contact, you can't see where they're headed next, until you feel a hand caressing the inside of your thigh, hear some shockingly filthy thoughts whispered in your ear, and feel a tongue in the place you least expected it.

5 HAVE A TONGUE TUSSLE

Did you honestly think I could write this without including some type of oral sex tip? Shame on you! While I could go on for hours about tongue technique for both of you, it does happen to be the most important part of it all. Practice makes perfect and, if you get this part right, the rest pales in comparison.

For him Concentrate your tongue action on the frenulum (the bit at the head of the penis on the underside, where the head meets the shaft). While your mouth is closed around his penis creating a warm, firm vacuum, make s-l-o-w circles around the rim of the head, giving a double lick and wiggle every time you pass the frenulum. Don't do it for too long if you're planning on intercourse afterward—he won't last that long!

RAUNCHRATING RAUNCHRATING
8/10
RAUNCH RAUNCHRATING

For her Instantly improve your oral sex technique by using the whole flat area of your tongue, rather than just the tip. Forget what you see in porn movies—they tense their tongue and stick it out so you see more action. Reality is different. Try it on your own palm and you'll see what I mean. First use the tip of your tongue to lick your palm. Note how it only stimulates a tiny area and can be quite rough. Now lay the whole top surface of your tongue flat against your palm. It covers a much larger area of skin and feels wetter, gentler, and softer. She's not the only one who'll benefit: your tongue is far less likely to get tired using it flat rather than pointed, because it's relaxed, not tensed.

RAUNCHRATING RAUNCHRATING
9/10
RAUNCH RAUNCHRATING

6 DRIVE HIM NUTS

For him Get ballsy by taking control of his. It is a bit of a personal thing—some men hate having their testicles stimulated; others love it—but it's definitely worth a shot. So often they're left shyly hanging

back there, while the star of the show, his penis, gets all the attention and affection. Be a fan: perfect your ball game and you hold the key to his sexual heaven in your hot little hands. Think of his testicles in the same way he thinks of your breasts. You can cradle them, suck them, stroke them, knead them. What you can't and shouldn't do, though, is bite or pull them too hard. They're often sensitive all over but have a good look the next time you're giving him oral sex. Search for a little ridge running up the middle, then follow it until you find the piece of skin that joins his testicles to his penis. This is usually the most sensitive part. It's best stimulated with your tongue, but use lubricant or your fingers (and saliva) and trace the area with your fingertips. Also try circling the area where the testicles and penis meet with the tip of your tongue, flicking it back and forth. Or use your tongue to lick swirling patterns around each testicle. Later, when you've started fellating him, you can use one hand to cup his testicles lightly and gently "juggle" them.

RAUNCHRATING RAUNCHRATING
7
10
RAUNCHRATING RAUNCHRATING

7 TURN IT UPSIDE DOWN

For both of you The upside-down 69er, invented by Alex Comfort (Mr. *Joy of Sex*), has never been bettered! She lies sideways across the bed and lowers her body to the floor, almost as though she's doing a handstand. Her head and palms rest on the floor; her legs and torso are still on the bed. He kneels on the bed, in between her legs. Because she's upside down, the pressure in the veins of the face and neck produce quite startling sensations. Don't like it? Then let yourself be tempted by some tantric: "The Crow" is the rather exotic name for the classic 69er position turned on its side: you both lie on your sides, head to toe, facing each other. Each of you draws your inner thigh up so it can be used as a cushion for your partner's head. It's a simple variation on the norm but a lot more comfortable for both of you.

8 COUNTDOWN TO ECSTASY

For him Finding it's all over a little faster than you'd both like? Count backward from 500 while having intercourse. Your brain's kept busy, so your penis is also distracted. Zero is blast off! Another technique, courtesy of sex therapist Carole Altman, enables you to isolate awareness of swelling in the penis and testicles and the movement of fluid. Do each step over one week: 1. Masturbate slowly, stopping as soon as you feel yourself getting erect; 2. Stroke until you get a slight erection, but go one or two strokes further; 3. Stroke but pay attention to feelings in the testicles. The minute you feel tightening and lifting, stop; 4. Stroke until conscious of testicle sensations, then try one or two strokes further; 5. Stroke until aware of the flow of semen in your penis, then with your thumb press hard on the vein running along the outside of the penis head.

RAUNCHRATING RAUNCHRATING **7/10**

RAUNCHRATING RAUNCHRATING **8/10**

9 TAKE A DETOUR

For him Can't have penetrative sex because you've got thrush/your period? Have "pretend" vaginal sex by lubricating his penis, keeping your thighs firmly together, and letting him thrust between them. Position yourself so his penis is sliding through the lips of your vagina, stimulating the clitoris, but no penetration is allowed. You can try this standing up, lying down, or from behind. Alternatively, try gluteal sex (from gluteus, the muscles of the buttocks): he applies lots of lubricant to his penis, you lie on your stomach and put a pillow

under your hips. He then thrusts between the cheeks of your buttocks. Or go "Spanish": oil your breasts and hold them firmly together as he thrusts in between.

RAUNCHRATING 7/10 RAUNCHRATING

10 VIBRATE WITH PLEASURE

Don't leave it shoved in the back of a drawer, rescued only when he's gone to a football game and you've got the house to yourself! Vibrators are the zero-effort, quick, and convenient way to orgasm if you're both tired or don't have much time.

For him Apply it to knotted, aching shoulders and the cheeks of his bottom before moving down to concentrate on the perineum—the area between his anus and testicles. Let him get used to the feeling before trying it out (on a low speed) on his testicles (cup them in one hand) and the opening of his anus. Depending on what sort of vibrator you have, you might like to insert it inside his rectum (definitely ask if the idea appeals first, though, and use tons of lubricant!), while giving him oral sex or masturbating him with your hands.

RAUNCHRATING 6/10 RAUNCHRATING

For her Again, use it on her shoulders, back, and feet, before moving to the obvious. Contrary to what the porn industry would have us believe, most women don't insert vibrators, but hold them firmly against the closed labia, sometimes massaging in small circles or using a press-then-lift motion, while applying varying pressure. She knows how she likes it, so it's a good idea to let her show you how it's done. After that, it's a weapon in your hands as you buzz, tease, and take her right to the brink…then back again (and again). Vibrators are terrific if she's horny and you're not, or you both want to orgasm but don't have the time or energy for anything that requires effort.

RAUNCHRATING 7/10 RAUNCHRATING

11 CREATE A FANTASY

For both of you Hate cell phones and computers? Bet you won't after this! Keep things steamy when you're apart by emailing or texting the first two sentences of a steamy fantasy, along with an instruction for them to send it back with the next two sentences added. Not only does it make that commute home a whole lot more interesting, but it's also a great way of coming up with fantasies that appeal to both of you, since both of you have equal input into what happens. Keep going back and forth with the game until you both come home to…turn it into reality, of course!

RAUNCHRATING RAUNCHRATING 8/10 RAUNCHRATING RAUNCHRATING

12 BE A SEX SLAVE

For both of you Be their sex slave for a day—yup, that's one entire day devoted to pleasuring them! They get to order you around—and whether it's making the bed or making whoopee, you're not allowed to utter even ONE word of complaint. Up the anticipatory factor by sending a card through the mail with the message "On (whatever date) I will be your sex slave for the entire day. Do with me what you will." That gives them plenty of time to think about what they're going to do with the time. Add three questions at the end: what do you want me to wear? (do you need to buy anything to fulfill the fantasy?); anything you crave, apart from me? (food, provisions, alcohol); anything else I need to make your dreams come true? (props if you're role-playing a fantasy). They don't need to forewarn you of what they've got planned (that would ruin the surprise), but the more they've thought about it, the better. There's nothing worse than having psyched yourself up into subservience, presented yourself as a slave, and then having your partner go bright red, shuffle their feet, and say "Uh, um, what would you like to do?"

RAUNCHRATING RAUNCHRATING 8/10 RAUNCHRATING RAUNCHRATING

Keep going **back and forth** with the game until you both come home to...**turn it into reality, of course!**

5 Sure-thing sex positions

If you're one of those women who can orgasm purely from intercourse then I'm very pleased for you. This is for the rest of us: the 90-odd percent of women who have the majority of our orgasms through oral sex or masturbation.

Not that we're complaining or jealous, mind you. OK, we are. Because as much as orgasms are delicious any way you can get them, it would be rather nice to have one during intercourse, when he's having his.

The point of these positions is to up your orgasm quota by hitting both internal and external hot spots. Never one to leave much to chance, I'd suggest we mount this campaign on two fronts: with words and action. Like, how about we debunk the myth and let him in on the secret, huh? You know, the one about the penis being the almighty satisfier. Because it's...well, rubbish really. Be honest. If you can only climax during intercourse when he's stroking your clitoris as well, tell him! Explain that it's not his fault but that lots of women are built that way and that it's a matter of biology, and has nothing to do with his sexual technique. If he's got a problem, tell him to take it up with God, or failing that, Mother Nature. Once he's recovered, give him a biology lesson.

He also gets to **watch the penis** go in and out, which is always up there on his **Things I'd Like To Do Today List.**

Does he know exactly where your clitoris is? Has he had a good look at it in broad daylight? Don't get all shy on me puhleeze! It's dark down there and it's easy to lose his bearings during different intercourse positions. I'm not saying that you lie down spread-eagle on the kitchen table just as the nextdoor neighbor stops by for morning coffee, but it is a very good idea to have the lights on at some point when he's giving you oral sex. Get him onside and clued up, then you can move on to trying your luck with these little gems. Now, I freely admit that one or two of these positions aren't just advanced but damn near impossible—unless you've got the flexibility of an acrobat and the body confidence of a supermodel. But never mind: you can always pretend this is what you get up to when sloshed at a dinner party! By the way, I've angled this section toward women, simply because it's easier to address one of you at a time when talking about legs facing this way and arms the other!

REINVENT OLD FAVORITES
Most couples have two or three favorite intercourse positions that, for whatever reasons, work best for them. While it's a good idea to push each other out of your comfort zones (and out of the bedroom!) to try

> I'm not saying you lie **spread-eagle on the kitchen table**, but it is a good idea to have the lights on at some point when **he's giving you oral sex.**

something new once in a while, reworking old favorites adds spice when you're not feeling quite as adventurous. Here's inspiration for the two most popular:

Lying positions
Zap life into the laziest lying position by going head to toe. This one's as simple as it gets. He lies on his back. Facing his feet, straddle his hips and lower yourself onto his erect penis. Then extend your legs

backward and lower your torso down until your feet are next to his head and you're lying on top of him. You're facing one way, and he's facing the other. His feet are near your head; your feet are near his. Try slow thrusting, so you can feel every inch of his penis as it slides slowly back and forth. For a different type of clitoral stimulation, slide off him for a second, look him straight in the…feet (i.e. feel free to fantasize like crazy!) and use your hand to slide the head of his penis up and

> # **Him-behind positions** leave your hands free to **stimulate his testicles** and perineum. It's also a great position to give yourself **a helping hand** at crucial points.

down to stroke your clitoris. Use your hand (or his) to continue to stimulate your clitoris manually while his penis is inside you—but stop just short of orgasm to let his thrusting trigger off the orgasm itself—and you've done what's officially called the "bridge maneuver." What this does is form a "bridge" between clitoral stimulation (how most women orgasm) and a penetrative orgasm (how men would like them to). Smart girl!

Girls on top
Ask him to sit up on the bed, his legs extended straight out in front of him. Climb on top, cowgirl style, and let him penetrate. Now fall back as far as you can until the top of your head is just resting on

TURN YOUR BACK ON HIM

The front wall of the vagina is incredibly sensitive—which is why rear-entry feels great for women. Here's three good reasons to sacrifice the benefits of face-to-face positions (like kissing) for other delights (orgasms). Thought I might convince you!

- **To activate a G-spot orgasm** Him-from-behind positions alter the angle of the vagina and give him a direct shot. Positions like The Swivel (see p.71) are ideal. Try to arch your back as far as you can, widening your legs so his penis has perfect access. If he's hitting the right spot and continues to thrust, the first reaction you'll have may be a need to pee because the G-spot is near the urethra (through which urine passes). Hang on (in all senses) and the sensation will pass and turn into an orgasmic wave that washes over you.
- **To get a good feel** Him-behind positions leave your hands free to stimulate his testicles and perineum (the smooth area between his testicles and anus). Meanwhile, he can stroke your back, bottom, and lower stomach. You get to set the pace and rhythm, to regulate the depth of penetration, and generally to be the dominant one. It's also a great position to give yourself a helping hand at crucial points because it's easy to reach down and stimulate your clitoris.
- **For fantasy paradise** There's no eye contact so both of you are free to fantasize about anyone and anything you like (without feeling guilty when opening one eye to see your partner gazing lovingly into yours). The rear-entry position is wonderfully primitive, so perfect for those slightly smutty, don't-even-admit-to-your-best-friend-type fantasies that suit "dirty" sex.

the bed. Reach backward with your hands until you can grasp his feet. Not only does your tummy look amazingly thin in this position, but it's also so easy to turn it into a killer workout if it suddenly reminds you that you should be at the gym, rather than lying around having sex. Instead of straddling him and resting on your knees, squat instead so your feet are on the bed. Stay leaning forward, then you do all the work—as in thrusting—and the only way to do

> **It's also so easy** to turn it into a **killer workout** if it suddenly reminds you that you should be at the gym, rather than **lying around having sex.**

this is to lift your heels and use those thigh muscles. Whatever, this position is bouncy, sexy sex—perfect for teasing him. Switch from fast up-and-down action before shifting gears and going for wide, circular motions. Will he like it? Excuse me? Your body is on full display so he gets to admire a full-frontal view because this position lays it all right out in front of him! He also gets to watch his penis go in and out, which is always up there on his Things I'd Like to Do Today List. (And one reason why this position is not such a great idea for Johnny-come-quickly's, because they'll lose it within seconds.) OK, now you've mastered the basics, it's time to tackle something a little more difficult. Try not to faint when you turn the page and see what's in store—most are actually easier than they first appear…

1 SIT-DOWN SEX

How to do it

He lies on his back and gets into the old "bicycle" exercise position (resting on his shoulders, his hips and bottom in the air, weight resting on his elbows, and hands holding hips high). You stand and face away from him and lower yourself onto his penis by sitting down on his bottom. His feet then rest against your back, while you rest your fingers on the back of his thighs for balance.

Why you'll love it

Yes, this one is a bit "wow!" His penis needs to be bent back and through his legs, which is why a semi-erection works best. Why attempt it? He might not love it but you will. You're in the driving seat (literally) so you can custom order your orgasm by controlling the depth of penetration and speed of thrusting.

2 THE HOOK

How to do it

You're lying on your back, he's on top. Hook your legs up over his shoulders for deeper penetration and to give him complete control.

Why you'll love it

If he's not terribly well-endowed, it's a good position for maximum deep penetration. A tip to remember for this and other positions: crossing your ankles (in this case behind his neck) helps tighten the vaginal canal. It's also a great way to squeeze him in and make him feel fuller inside you. The scrotum brushes against your buttocks with each stroke. You can reach forward to stroke or cup his testicles, while he can do wonderful things to your breasts with his hands. The blood will have rushed to extremities like your nipples, which makes them highly sensitive.

3 THE SLIDE
How to do it

He kneels on a hard surface, keeping his back straight. You lie in front of him, genitals facing him. He then lifts your legs up to his shoulders, so your weight is supported on your shoulders. Holding his erection downward, he then penetrates you. He holds you in position by wrapping his arms around your upper thighs.

Why you'll love it

This works because he penetrates shallowly. And—gosh! how tactful is Mother Nature!—all the vaginal nerve endings are located within an inch or so of the vaginal entrance. The reason this position works: he's focusing on your super-sensitive nerve endings with what also happens to be his most sensitive part—the head of his penis.

4 THE SWIVEL

How to do it

You're on top, then, through a series of moves, you turn around while he's still inside you and end up facing the opposite way. So start by riding him rodeo style. Then, using your hands to steady yourself, lift one leg over his body and begin to turn sideways. Continue rotating, stopping at intervals for a few thrusts, until you're facing away from him.

Why you'll love it

He gets a unique corkscrew feeling on his penis while you turn around, and is simultaneously treated to a revolving-restaurant-type view of your body. His erection points out instead of up, which is an instant arousal upper. You can vary the thrusting to make things even more interesting. Grind into him slowly, then suddenly speed up, or vary the depth of penetration.

5 UPSIDE-DOWN SEX
How to do it

Both stand facing each other.
You jump up and wrap your legs
around his waist and arms around
his neck. Let him penetrate, then
very slowly and carefully let go and
let your body fall backward until
you're in a handstand position with
your palms on the floor, facing
away from him. He supports you
by holding your waist and buttocks.
Yes, you do need to be flexible but
it's actually not as difficult as it
sounds (and you've got to admit,
it looks damn impressive!).

Why you'll love it

It's called inversion: him
taking you head down.
Because the blood literally
rushes to your head, it
builds pressure in the veins
of the face and neck,
producing startling
sensations on orgasm.
Oh, and it's great for
your balance and gives
your abs a workout.

6 THE INTERLOCK

How to do it

Start by getting into the missionary position. He then sits up and brings both legs forward, one at a time, so the soles of his feet are flat on the bed. His knees are bent and he's facing you. He then leans back and supports himself on his hands. You sit up and do the same. Put your ankles on his shoulders and lift your hips as high as possible.

Why you'll love it

This position's good for aiming at the A-spot (the Anterior Fornex Erogenous). This hot spot was accidentally discovered in 1996 by scientists trying to find a cure for vaginal dryness. They were astonished to find that 95 percent of women became massively turned on when this area was stimulated. It's a smooth, extremely sensitive spot halfway between your G-spot and your cervix.

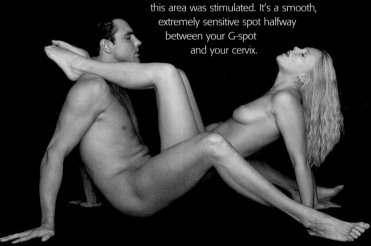

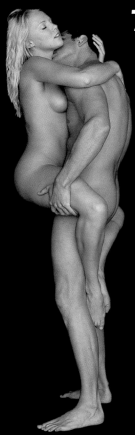

7 THE WALL THRUST

How to do it

You lean with your back against a wall, and he stands in front of you. Now jump up and wrap your legs around his waist and put your arms around his neck, keeping your back and head against the wall for stability. He penetrates in this position, legs apart, hands holding on to your thighs and bottom.

Why you'll love it

Because he's holding you, he feels a real sense of power and potency. He can also maintain an erection for longer when standing up because the blood is needed elsewhere in his body, so his erection isn't as intense. This isn't altogether bad news. It means he's in control enough to spend time concentrating on your pleasure and the slow teasing and buildup makes his orgasm positively explosive when it does actually happen.

8 THE STARFISH

How to do it

You both lie on the bed, heads in opposite directions. Scissor your legs so he can penetrate, then hang on to each other's hands for leverage.

Why you'll love it

This technique is perfect for achieving a grinding pressure movement, advocated by the CAT (Coital Alignment Technique). Given that the in-out, in-out motion of thrusting during intercourse does little to keep the pressure constant on the clitoris—which is what's needed for orgasm—the CAT technique works on the principle that instead of moving apart, you should push your hips together and maintain pressure on the clitoris as you rock back and forth. (Purrrr!) Arch your backs and move away from each other to allow deeper penetration or adjust the angle so he's hitting the right spots.

6 **Best sex ever**

Shelve your inhibitions along with that book and get ready for a serious lust injection.

SEXUAL FANTASY

Sexperts used to argue that no one could become sexually aroused without being touched. Good luck finding anyone these days who won't agree that it's possible to arouse yourself using only your mind. Which is, by the way, great news for any couple in love who want to go the distance. Just about everyone has amused themselves on a plane/train/bus by imagining what the stranger sitting across from them would look like naked (on your lap, in your bed, over that convenient railing…). Sounds weird, I know, but this is actually great news. While you may run out of new positions/places/props/techniques/ideas (in about 20 years), there's one thing that is limitless: your imagination. When the urge to play and stray strikes (and it will—it always does), fantasy and role-playing are lovely ways of having the best of both worlds. By having the affair in your head, it boosts your sex life with your partner, giving it the spicy edge it needs to solve the sexual frustration of monogamy, without the hurtful complications of a real-life affair. Does this mean that most fantasies are better left in our imaginations? Quite frankly, yes! Most aren't meant to be brought to life (though there are exceptions—keep reading). As my favorite ago, advice columnist, Irma Kurtz of *Cosmo*, puts it, most fantasies are by definition the free play of creative imagination: fiction, fakery, unreality. The whole point of them is that they're not real life. Take out the forbidden factor by making them real and you nearly always remove the appeal (not to mention get yourself into a whole lot of trouble). Many women have rape fantasies. This does not mean we want to be raped. Some men have same-sex fantasies. It does not necessarily

> "Honey, do you mind terribly if **I call you Dr. Vincent during sex?** You know, the doctor from the **practice down the street?**"

make them gay. Some women get massively turned on imagining their partner having sex with another woman. In reality, he'd be castrated. I'm with Irma, who says: if you're not 100 percent convinced it'll be a huge success, don't force it to survive the transition to reality.

ROLE-PLAYING
Ah-ha! Didn't I just say not to take fantasy through to reality? Well...yes. But I did say there were exceptions—and this is what I mean. It's one thing to bonk the much-lusted-after local doctor or tell your partner you'd like to; it's quite another to live out a sexy scenario where you're both playing roles. Here's the difference: "Honey, do

you mind terrily if I call you Dr. Vincent during sex? You know, the doctor from the practice down the street. Well, he's the guy who does my PAP smears and breast checks. And he's just soooooo dishy! Every time I have sex with you, I fantasize you're him anyway, and if I could say 'Yes! Yes! Harder Dr. Vincent!' it would make it seem even more real. You don't mind, do you honey?...Honey?" Compare this to: "Honey, how about we play an X-rated version of doctors and nurses?" Exactly.

Here's how to transform your risky fantasy into risqué role-playing. First, get the general plot in your head. It's easier if you divide it into four parts: 1. Where/how you meet; 2. What happens when you do; 3. How it all starts happening; 4. What happens when it does (most detail here). Make it real by thinking about:

WHERE you should do it It's very useful to role-play away from home (like on a dirty weekend) because it's much easier to pretend that you're someone else when you're not in familiar surroundings, which bring on familiar roles.

Do you LOOK the part? Role-playing works best if you give your partner an instant visual jolt when they see you. Seeing you dressed as someone else forces them to see you "anew"—as if they don't know you. (Especially effective if you've turned into best friends who bonk, by the way.) What clothes do you need to buy/rent? Are there any other changes you need to make to your appearance to fit the part? Wigs are fantastic: they change your look so dramatically, you feel like a completely different person the instant you put them on. It's far easier to get into character as a blonde bimbette if you've got

the long blonde hair to go with it. Or turn into a doctor when you've got the stethoscope. Masks also work, for the same reason. They're something to hide behind.

How to ACT? You've got the plot and the look, now work on the attitude! Get into character. Think of three adjectives you would use to describe the personality of the character you're playing. What about your partner? If you're in charge of the fantasy, give them specific instruction—or at least some clues—on how you want them to behave in their role. Below are two (ever-popular) scenarios to get those brain cells firing:

- **The sex worker** She wears super-revealing (OK, slutty) clothes under a big coat. You drop her off on a street corner (chosen carefully for obvious reasons). Park up the street and watch her, pretending she's a sex worker. Then cruise up, wind the window down, call her over, and ask how much. Get her to unbutton her coat and show you what you're getting for your hard-earned cash. Negotiate before she gets in. On the way (home/somewhere remote) tell her what you want her to do, and she'll tell you what she'll give you for the price. Keep everything cold/hard/impersonal (emphasis on hard).

- **Pick-me-up** Choose the type of venue you'd go to if you were looking to pick someone up (a bar?), then plant your partner there. Get him to strike a pose—as in, settle where he would if he were, in real life, single. Then, you make your move, i.e. blatantly pick him up for a wicked one-night stand. Yes, you'll both want to laugh and whatever you say will sound contrived. But, hello! I bet a box of chocolates that you both really did say that sort of stuff when you first met. You can play it as a repeat of your first night together or be two strangers who pass like ships in the night.

REVISIT the fantasy…instantly by deciding on a code word. If you were "Jane/Jake" during the role-playing, saying "I bet Jane/Jake would love that" is your cue for both of you to go back into character.

BLINDFOLDS

…are excellent for helping to create the right atmosphere for role-playing—particularly if you're rotten actors. They reduce embarrassment and increase awareness of physical sensations because you're closing off one sense, which highlights all the others. You can't anticipate what's in store next, so are forced to stay in a perpetual state of excitement. Poor thing.

While **you may run out** of new positions/ places/**props/techniques**/ideas (in about 20 years), there's **one thing that is limitless**: your imagination.

The shy dominatrix Blindfold him, lead him into the bedroom, tie his hands behind his back, and get him to lie on the bed. Now, take him to the brink of orgasm and back again, time and time again. Kiss him. Rub your breasts against his chest, let him take a nipple in his mouth, then remove it (almost) immediately. Lower yourself over him for oral sex, let him smell you, then lift off again. Later, let him give a few licks, then get off (I know, it's hard). When he is hard, lower yourself over his throbbing manhood (I'm sorry but I just had to get

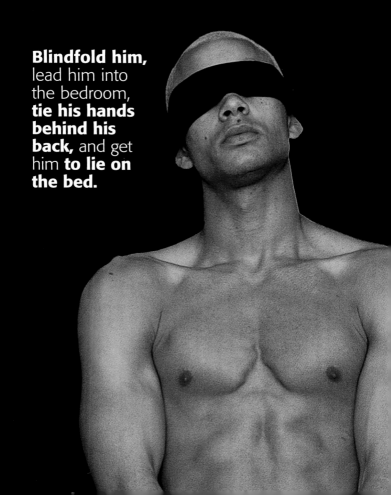

Blindfold him, lead him into the bedroom, **tie his hands behind his back,** and get him **to lie on the bed.**

that phrase in somewhere) and let him penetrate, then climb off almost immediately. Follow that with the best kissing he's ever had, but no body contact. Then go back and do it all over again, but each time a bit longer. When you've brought him to boiling point several times—at least three "almosts"—climb on top and let him climax.

Always **keep your spanks** on the too light side rather than too heavy and **ask her to say "harder"** to up the pressure.

SPANKING

One in 10 men fantasize about spanking a woman's bottom and one in 20 wishes she'd do it to him. The statistics for women aren't as clear-cut, but it's certainly a popular fantasy.

Indulge her by... Pulling down her skirt/pants but leave it/them around her knees (part of the game is the humiliation), then bend her over your knee. Warm up the buttocks first by kneading them firmly, as though they were dough, throwing in a few light, playful slaps. Start to get firmer and heavier and play cheek to cheek, like her bottom is a set of drums. Vary your strokes so you're mixing light with quick, firm smacks. Alternate with teasing touches when you brush your fingers between her legs. If she seems to enjoy it, introduce props: the back of a hairbrush; the bottom of a pair of shoes; a wooden spoon. Always keep your spanks on the too light side rather than too heavy and ask her to say "harder" to up the pressure.

BONDAGE

Being tied up and in control are mutually exclusive—hence the appeal to stressed-out business types who (statistically) relish bondage games and not having to be the boss. It's also appealing to women hung up on the good-girls-don't issue: with the loss of control comes removal of responsibility, a gift that removes blame, guilt, and inhibition even quicker than it removes clothes. Others love it just because it's wicked (and you get to play dress-up).

> **Most fantasies** are by definition the free play of creative imagination: **fiction, fakery, unreality.** The whole point of them is that they're **not real life.**

How to transform yourself from Ms. Butter-Wouldn't-Melt-in-My-Mouth to Madame Lash *The look*: ditch the lace for leather—preferably black or red. Chokers work well. Think tight and clingy rather than loose and flowing: lace-up boots and corsets, the higher and spikier the shoes, the better. *The personality*: start initiating sex more and taking more control. You get on top and stay there. Keep your top and bra on and if he tries to remove it, say "No!" forcefully and pin his hands down on either side of his head. Ride him mercilessly. *Action*: by now, he should be getting the drift of things. Use your (worn) stockings to tie his wrists behind his back. If he's not complaining at this point, he's yours to do with as you will…

Think tight and clingy rather than loose and flowing: **lace-up boots and corsets,** the higher and **spikier the shoes,** the better.

...AND WHEN YOU'VE DONE ALL THOSE, GIVE THESE A WHIRL

- **Buy a case of his favorite wine** and wrap 12 notes around the neck of each bottle, detailing things you're planning to do to him as you're sharing the wine.

- **Challenge her to a game of sexual scrabble.** Follow the normal rules but all the words have to be connected to sex. Make sure you spell out deliberate messages about what you'd like to do to her once the game's over.

- **Let him play peeping Tom.** Pretend to undress and masturbate as though you're alone but let him watch you.

- **Book a weekend at a sexy luxury hotel.** Wrap up the brochure with a handwritten weekend itinerary of what you intend to do to her.

- **Write sexy notes** and leave them in unexpected places. Like stuck on a bottle of beer in the refrigerator/on the bathroom mirror/in his wallet ("If you were here now, I'd be on my knees."). Confess your most erotic fantasy—and promise to do it.

- **Roll with it:** *Cosmo's* come up with a winner in Vice-Dice: you need three to decide what you'll be doing sexually that night. Die one decides where (kitchen table, the car, in front of the window with lights on). Die two decides what (particular position, oral sex, masturbation). Die three decides what with (a blindfold, bondage, a camera).

- **The way to keep anyone interested in anything is to do what's least expected.** No matter how amazing a sexual maneuver, it'll be about as exciting as doing the dishes if it's always delivered in the same way. Capture the spirit of unpredictability and you'll be the favorite for the Most Valued Lover Award.

REAL COUPLES REVEAL ALL

Most of us, sadly, are on first-name terms with so-so sex. Thankfully, also for most, this is balanced by a fair smattering of great sex sessions as well. But what about exceptional sex? When you didn't just go to heaven, but you were introduced to God and got his autograph. What are the ingredients that make sex truly unforgettable? I asked a mix of real people to look at a lifetime of intimacy and 'fess up the naughtiest parts. Here's a selection of their trips down most-memorable lane to find the sexperience they'll never quite forget. What made their finest sexual hour (or so) so special? Read carefully, you might just pick up a thing or two...

THE S-L-O-W TEASE

"I'd just come out of a really heavy long-term relationship and met this guy at a boozy lunch at a friend's house. He was definitely not my type long-term (not the sharpest knife in the drawer) but he had a body to die for and a great sense of humor. Over the next six weeks we hung out together and flirted like mad, but I felt too raw emotionally to sleep with him. Instead, we'd kiss and touch (no naughty parts) and it turned into the most deliciously drawn-out sexual tease I've ever had. Toward the end, I was so turned on, all he had to do was kiss my neck and I'd practically orgasm! It was worth the wait: when I was finally ready, he led me into the bedroom and we didn't come out for 10 hours."

What made it great   "It had all the essentials, which I call 'the three Ts': tease, talk, technique. The build-up was extraordinary but it also helped that he was incredibly nonjudgmental and I felt comfortable talking to him about sex. He'd obviously been around the block a few times because he knew exactly what he was doing. Also, it was no-strings sex with an expiration date. The pressure of being Ms. Pure was lifted because I wasn't auditioning as wife material and I was able to let loose completely, which meant that I could just focus on the sex."

SWING CITY

"I'd been trying to talk my girlfriend into going to a swingers' club for years. I could see the idea appealed, but she was paranoid about people finding out so we decided to do it while on vacation. Upstairs it looked like a normal club, but downstairs was a vista of mattresses, benches, love seats, semicurtained rooms, and mirrors. They called it the 'private' area—but it was anything but. I lifted her skirt, pulled aside the flimsy G-string she was hardly wearing and sank into her. The intensity was indescribable: the waiting, the wanting, the illegality, the not knowing if someone would come in and find us in full swing. Usually our lovemaking is long, varied, always deeply passionate, stretching over an hour or more. This time it lasted minutes. Later on, she danced with some guy and let him feel her up, in public, on the dancefloor. I danced with a girl who looked like Cleopatra who rubbed my penis inside my pants, kissed my mouth, and allowed me full access to her vagina. The feeling of sliding my fingers along her clitoris, into the slight separation between her labia and onto her vagina was intense, made even more intense as I watched my girlfriend being fondled by the guy she was dancing with. But when he sank to his knees and lifted her skirt to give her oral sex, she came back to me, inserted herself between me and Cleopatra and, looking me fully in the eye, said 'No.' Limits reached, we went home after that—to bonk ourselves stupid!"

What made it great "It was just so kinky. Not only did we get to watch other people having sex—real people, not pathetic porn actors—but also having full permission to make love to another woman, in front of her, was amazing. It's the complete opposite to what normally happens. Most girlfriends freak if you even look at other women, let alone touch them. I don't know how I would have felt watching her have full-blown sex with the guy, but watching them kiss and fondle was sexy."

EX SEX

"My ex-boyfriend showed up to take me out. I wasn't sure whether it was now friendship or if he was trying to get together again. But I did know I was as horny as hell. Anyway, all that stuff about pheromones must be true because after the briefest talk at the door, he made a joke about me looking good and wanting to ravish me, then said 'In fact, I will,' picked me up, and headed for the bedroom. We were both laughing when he threw me on the bed but then the mood changed. He started kissing and he told me (in graphic detail) exactly what he wanted to do to me last time we went out but was too scared to suggest it. It's actually unlike him to indulge in dirty talk but I loved it! I asked him what he'd have liked me to do to him and he said give him more blow-jobs. So I did. Then he asked me to masturbate for him and I did, while he watched, masturbating himself at the same time. We got up to all kinds of things—kinky stuff I'd never done before—and, to be honest, haven't done since. Sadly."

What made it great "We broke up because I thought he was a bit of a drip and too much in touch with his feminine side. I was always the one in control of the relationship, so him taking charge sexually, and really forcefully, was a surprise. It blew me away! It was the role-reversal combined with feeling safe enough to confess all these wicked fantasies that made it so hedonistic."

THE BEST OF THE REST…
For him

"Squeezing my testicles, just before orgasm."

"Watching her play with herself. She'd look me straight in the eye as she did it."

"She'd insert her finger up my bottom while giving me oral sex."

"Giving me a blow-job while I was driving."

"Watching in mirrors above us, beside us, she had them placed everywhere."

"She used to bite my nipples hard, just as I was about to let go."

"Her tongue darting inside my anus."

"Her giving me head in a public place—the thrill of thinking we might be caught."

"She'd squirt lots of lube into her palms and rub them together, then masturbate me."

"Ordering me to climax in her mouth instead of trying to avoid it."

"Expecting to see pubes and then the sight of her totally shaved genitals."

For her

"Being blindfolded and then feeling his tongue everywhere."

"Kissing another woman while he watched."

"Realizing I had complete and utter control over him: physically and emotionally."

"The freedom to let loose and not caring if he judged me."

"Being the boss, ordering him around, treating him like a slave—like dirt, actually."

"Having a guy so fast after meeting him, I didn't even know his name—or want to find out."

"Talking dirty and saying all the stuff a female's not supposed to."

"Giving in to lust, which didn't have a 'possible future relationship' tag on it."

"I can't decide which was better—the totally unexpected sexual encounter or the eagerly anticipated one that followed."

"Him making lots of noise while going down on me."

"Lots of creative foreplay, gentle then rough, and I didn't ever want it to stop."

Index

Acknowledgments

All photography by John Davis
DK would like to thank Laurence Errington for the index.